LADY ANTEBELLUM

Album artwork and photography © 2008 Capitol Records Nashville
Photographers: Andrew Southam, Chris Hicky, and C. Taylor Crothers
Album package graphic design: Matt Taylor

Alfred Music Publishing Co., Inc.
16320 Roscoe Blvd., Suite 100
P.O. Box 10003
Van Nuys, CA 91410-0003
alfred.com

ISBN-10: 0-7390-6264-6
ISBN-13: 978-0-7390-6264-7

Love Don't Live Here

I really felt like we found our sound on this song, and I was really proud that it became our first single since it was one of the first songs that the three of us wrote together. —Charles

Lookin' for a Good Time

We tried not to take ourselves too seriously on this one! And we've all had a story like this, right? —Dave

ALL WE'D EVER NEED

This was the very first song the three of us wrote together. The funny thing is, it would have never been a duet if I had never begged Charles to put his voice on it... which led to Lady Antebellum. —Hillary

Long Gone

I wrote this song "pre-Lady Antebellum" but we all felt like it fit this project perfectly. The lyrics in this song are very empowering and I think every woman, including myself, can relate to this. —Hillary

I Run to You

This song is an expression against hate, prejudice, negativity, running the rat race, but ultimately the redemption of love! And it has an irresistible melody and a head-bobbing groove. What could be better? —Paul Worley

Love's Lookin' Good on You

This is just a fun, good-feelin' love song and the first time the band heard it they said "WE HAVE TO HAVE THAT SONG!" Being that Charles is 6' 6" and was barring the door I pretty much had no choice. And the rest, as they say, is history! —Victoria Shaw

Home Is Where The Heart Is

I remember finding this song as a rough demo on my iPod by accident, and thinking "Gosh how did we forget about this one?!" —Dave

THINGS PEOPLE SAY

The day Charles and I wrote this song, we went for pizza that night with some friends, and after dinner I was walking to my car to grab the CD that had the song on it to show our friends. Right after I got the CD out of the car I was approached by four men who tried to take my car keys, one punched me in the face, one held a fake gun to my back (I think it was fake!), but luckily I got away....oh and the CD was still in my left hand, no scratches :) True story. —Dave

SLOW DOWN SISTER

I really love the intro to this song, and it's become one of our favorites to do live. We actually added the bridge while recording it in the studio. —Charles

Can't Take My Eyes Off You

This was the second song the three of us wrote together. I remember sitting on the couch with Charles watching Dave add mandolin to the initial demo. The lights were down low and I remember having this romantic feeling come over me and that we had written something really special.

—Hillary

One Day You Will

This song was a real departure for us as writers. We usually tend to write about relationships. It was nice to write a song that inspired and uplifted us, and hopefully it'll do the same for you. —Charles

CONTENTS

LOVE DON'T LIVE HERE

Words and Music by
DAVE HAYWOOD, CHARLES KELLEY
and HILLARY SCOTT

C(9)
G
F6/9
1.
C(9)
D♭(9)
A♭
G♭6/9
D♭(9)
to get back what is gone. But I'm
oh, and I would curse your name.
2. C(9)
G
F6/9
C(9)
D♭(9)
A♭
G♭6/9
D♭(9)
Hey!
G
F6/9
C(9)
Verses 2 & 3:
G
F6/9
A♭
G♭6/9
D♭(9)
A♭
G♭6/9
2. Well, I heard the news
you can try
C(9)
G
F6/9
C(9)
D♭(9)
A♭
G♭6/9
D♭(9)
that you were back in town and just
to tell me how it is, and try to

G
F6/9
C(9)
A♭
G♭6/9
D♭(9)
pass - ing through
jus - ti - fy
to claim your lost and found.
ev - 'ry - thing you did.
But I'm o - ver you,
But, hon-ey, I'm no fool,
and
and
there ain't noth - ing that
I've been down this road
you could say or do
too man - y times with you,
to take what you did back.
and I think it's best you go.
Well,
Well,

D
E♭
F
G♭
you got nerve__ to waltz__ right in__ and think what's mine__ is yours__
I got one__ thing left__ to say:__ You could lay in the bed__
Chorus:
G
A♭
__ a - gain.__
__ you made.__
'Cause I've been do - in' fine with - out__ you,
Am7
B♭m7
C
D♭
for - get - tin' all the love we once__ knew.__ And, girl, I ain't the
F
G♭
G
A♭
F
G♭
C
D♭
one that slammed__ that door.__

G
A♭
Am7
B♭m7
Now you'll see a change in think - in'. Well, I ain't got a
C
D♭
F
G♭
heart for break - in', so go and pick your bags up off my floor.
G
A♭
F
G♭
Whoa, 'cause love don't live
C(9)
D♭(9)
1.
G
A♭
F6/9
G♭6/9
C(9)
D♭(9)
G
A♭
F6/9
G♭6/9
here an - y - more, no, no.

2.
C(9)
Db(9)
G
Ab
N.C.
3. Well, ba-by,
oh, no.
That love
don't live here an-y-more.
F6/9
Gb6/9
Whoa, no, no.
Sug-ar, no,
no.
You don't live here an-

C(9)
G
F6/9
C(9)
D♭(9)
A♭
G♭6/9
D♭(9)
y - more.
Love don't live___ here an - y - more.
Since you walked_ out of___ my door,_
love don't live___ here, love_
___ don't live___ here, girl.___
Oh, love_
___ don't live___ here an - y - more.___

LOOKIN' FOR A GOOD TIME

Words and Music by
CHARLES KELLEY, DAVE HAYWOOD,
HILLARY SCOTT and KEITH FOLLESE

*Female lead vocal only 1st time.
Male harmony (in cues) added 2nd time.

C(9)
G(9)
hang - ing on your ev - 'ry word.
band is good, the mu - sic's loud. But
D
Am
Keep those drinks a - com - ing, may - be
would you get the wrong im - pres - sion if
C(9)
D
we'll both get what we de - serve.
I called us a cab right now?
Chorus:
G
Dsus
Am
C(9)
G
D
How 'bout, ba - by, we make a prom - ise to not prom - ise an - y - thing

F
C(9)
G
Dsus
Am
C(9)
more than one night? Com - pli - cat - ed sit - u - a - tions
G
D
Am7
D
To Coda
on - ly get worse in the morn - ing light.
1.
N.C.
G
G/B
C2
G
G/B
C2
Hey, I'm just look - in' for a good time.
G
G/B
C2
G
G/B
C2
2.
N.C.
2. Put in a long,
Hey, I'm just look - in' for a

G
G/B
C2
good_ time.
(Inst. solo ad lib....
...end solo)
Bridge:
Am
Male:
Go a-head and lie to me and pull me close.
Female:
Tell___ me that you love me e-ven
if you don't._
Both:
The rule is: Don't you ev-er e-ven talk a-bout for-ev-er, but you
nev-er say nev-er in life.
D
Dsus
D.S. 𝄋 al Coda

Coda
G
G/B
C2
Hey, I'm just look - in' for a good time.
Hey, I'm just look - in' for a
good time.

ALL WE'D EVER NEED

Words and Music by
DAVE HAYWOOD, CHARLES KELLEY
and HILLARY SCOTT

*All vocals are written at pitch.

Em
E♭+
G/D
C♯m7(♭5)
I stare at your pho - to - graph,
still sleep in the shirt you left.
Am7
D
G
C/G
G
D/F♯
And no - bod - y knows it but me.
Ev - 'ry
Em
D
C(9)
day, I wipe my tears a - way.
So man - y
Em
D
F(9)
nights I've prayed for you to say...

Chorus:
G
G/B
C(9)
D
Both:
Female:
I should have been chas - ing you.
I should have been try'n' to prove that
mf
Em
D
C(9)
D
you were all that mat - tered to me.
G
G/B
C(9)
D
Both:
I should have said all the things
that I kept in - side of me, and
Em
D
C(9)
G/B
Female:
may - be I could have made you be - lieve
that

Am7 G/B C(9)

what we had___ was all___ we'd___ ev - er need.___

G D/G C/G

Verse 2:

Em E♭+ G/D C♯m7(♭5)

Male:

2. My friends_ think I'm mov - ing on,___ but the truth is,___ I'm not that strong.

Am7 Dsus G C/G G D/F♯

And no - bod - y knows___ it___ but me.___

Em
Eb+
G/D
C#m7(b5)
And I've kept all the words you said in a box un - der - neath my bed.
Am7
D
G
C/G
G
D/F#
Both:
And no - bod - y knows it but me.
But if you're
Em
D
C(9)
hap - py, I'll get through some - how,
but the
Em
D
F(9)
Male:
truth is that I've been scream - ing out.

Chorus:
G
G/B
C(9)
D
Both:
Male:
I should have been chas - ing you.
I should have been try'n' to prove that
Em
D
C(9)
D
you were all that mat - tered to me.
G
G/B
C(9)
D
Both:
Male:
I should have said all the things that I kept in - side of me, and
Em
D
C(9)
G/B
Both:
may - be I could have made you be - lieve that

Am7
G/B
C(9)
what we had was all we'd ev - er need.
Em7
D
Male:
It was all we'd ev - er need.
C(9)
Em7
D
Female:
Oh, I thought it was all we'd ev - er need.
C(9)
Em7
D
(Guitar solo ad lib....

Am7
G/B
C(9)
…end solo)
G
G/B
C(9)
D
Male:
I should have been chas - ing you.
Female:
You should have been try'n' to prove
Male:
that
Em
D
C(9)
D
you were all that mat - tered to me.
G
G/B
C(9)
D
Female:
You should have said all the things
Male:
that I kept in - side of me,
Female:
and

Em
D
C(9)
G/B
Male:
may - be you could-'ve made me be - lieve that
Am7
G/B
C(9)
G/B
Female:
what we had, girl...
Oh, that what
Am7
G/B
C(9)
Em7
Male:
Both:
we had,
What we had,
it was all we'd ev - er need.
mp
Dsus
C(9)
Em7
F
It was all we'd ev - er need.
poco rit.

LONG GONE

Words and Music by
KEITH FOLLESE, ADRIENNE FOLLESE,
HILLARY SCOTT and VICTORIA SHAW

Moderately ♩ = 112

Guitar Capo 2 ⟶ Em7 G D5

Piano ⟶ F♯m7 A E5

mf

Em7 G D5
F♯m7 A E5

Em7 G D5
F♯m7 A E5

Em7 G D5
F♯m7 A E5

Verse:

Em7 G D5 Em7 G
F♯m7 A E5 F♯m7 A

1. It's so like you just to show up at my door and act like
2. Don't waste your breath with __ "Ba - by, ba - by, please." 'Cause I am

*All vocals written at pitch.

D5
E5
Em7
F♯m7
G
A
D5
E5
noth - ing's hap - pened. You think I'll sweep my heart up off the
so not lis - t'nin'. Don't both - er get - ting down up - on your
C(9)
D(9)
Am7
Bm7
floor and give it to you like so man - y times be - fore.
knees and try to beg me, I'm tired of how you twist the truth.
C(9)
D(9)
You're talk - ing to a strang - er. I'm not that girl an - y - more.
You're not talk - ing to the same girl who used to for - give
D
E
Chorus:
G
A
you.
That girl is long

C(9)
D(9)
D
E
gone. Boy, you missed the boat, it just sailed a - way.
G
A
C(9)
D(9)
D
E
Long gone, she's not drown - ing in her
Am7
Bm7
G/B
A/C♯
yes - ter - days. Bet you nev - er thought I'd be that strong.
1.
C(9)
D(9)
D
E
Em7
F♯m7
Well, this girl is long

G
D
A
E
gone.
2.
C(9)
D
Bridge:
C(9)
D(9)
E
D(9)
Well, this girl is gone like the wind un - der
G/B
A/C♯
Su - per-man's cape. Like a thief in the night, I made the great es - cape. I'm not the
F(9)
D
G(9)
E
kind of girl that keeps mak - ing the same mis - takes.

Chorus:

G C(9) Dsus D
A D(9) Esus E

That girl is long gone. Boy, you missed_ the boat,_ it just

G C/G Dsus D
A D/A Esus E

sailed_ a - way._ Long gone, I'm not drown-ing in_ my

Am7 G/B C(9)
Bm7 A/C♯ D(9)

yes - ter - days._ Bet you nev - er thought_ I'd be_ that strong._ Bet you did-

Am7 G/B C(9)
Bm7 A/C♯ D(9)

n't. Yeah, well, ba - by, I proved_ you wrong._

D
G
C(9)
D
E
A
D(9)
E
This girl is long gone, long gone.
G
C(9)
D
A
D(9)
E
This girl is long gone, long gone.
G
C(9)
A
D(9)
This girl is long gone.
D
G
E
A
This girl is gone.

I RUN TO YOU

Words and Music by
CHARLES KELLEY, DAVE HAYWOOD,
HILLARY SCOTT and TOM DOUGLAS

Gtr. tuned down 1/2 step:
⑥ = E♭ ③ = G♭
⑤ = A♭ ② = B♭
④ = D♭ ① = E♭

E
Bsus
F♯m7(4)
E♭
B♭sus
Fm7(4)
u - dice. I___ run from pes - si - mists,_ but I run___ too___ late.__
Verses 2 & 3:
A2
E
Bsus
Verse 2 (sing 1st time only):
A♭2
Female:
E♭
B♭sus
2. I run___ my___ life,_
Verse 3 (sing 2nd time only):
on___ fumes._
F♯m7(4)
A(9)
E
Fm7(4)
A♭(9)
E♭
___ or is it run - nin' me? Run from my past,___ I___ run too fast_
Your_ life and mine,___ like the sands of time,_

Bsus
B♭sus
F♯m7(4)
Fm7(4)
A(9)
A♭(9)
Both:
or too slow, it seems.
When
Our
slip-pin' right on through.
mf
B
B♭
F♯m7
Fm7
lies be - come the truth,
love's the on - ly truth,
B
B♭
that's when I run to you.
that's why I run to you.

Chorus:
F♯m7
Fm7
B7
B♭7
E
E♭
This world_ keeps
B
B♭
spin - nin' fast - er in - to a new__ di - sas - ter, so I run
F♯m7
Fm7
E
E♭
to you,____ I run to you, ba - by. And when it all____ starts
B
B♭
com - in' un - done, ba - by, you're the on - ly one I run_

F#m7
Fm7
1.
E
E♭
to.
I run to you.
mp
Bsus
B♭sus
F#m7(4)
Fm7(4)
A(9)
A♭(9)
Both:
3. We run
2.
Bridge:
A
A♭
E/G#
E♭/G
B
B♭
C#m
Cm
Male:
I run to you.
Whoa, whoa.
Female:
Oh, I run to you.

B
C♯m
F♯m7
B
B♭
Cm
Fm7
B♭
Chorus:
E
Both:
E♭
B
B♭
This world keeps spin - nin' fast - er in - to a new di -
F♯m7
Fm7
sas - ter, so I run to you, I run to you, ba - by.
E
E♭
B
B♭
And when it all starts com - in' un - done, ba - by, you're the

F♯m7
Fm7
Female:
on - ly one I run to. I run
A
A♭
Both:
B
B♭
E
E♭
to you, I run to you, yeah.
Male:
B
B♭
Female:
Whoa, whoa. Oh, I run to you.
F♯m7
Fm7
Male:
Male:
A
A♭
I run to you, girl. Whoa.

B/A
A
Bb/Ab
Ab
Male:
I al - ways run to you.
Female:
Run to you.
Female:
Run to you.
mp

LOVE'S LOOKIN' GOOD ON YOU

Words and Music by
MATT LOPEZ,
JASON DEERE
and VICTORIA SHAW

D
some - thing's changed that I can't quite put my fin - ger on.
Well, I've been
kind of makes you think that the stars were in sync on the night we met.
There ought-ta
F♯m
E
D
rack-in' my brain. Wait just a min-ute. Hold on now. Well, I get it.
be a red car-pet ev-'ry-where you go. Roll it on out. Hey, don't you know that...
Chorus:
A
D
E
Love, love, love's look-in' good, good, good on you.

A
D
E
Well, can you feel it? Oh, ev - 'ry - bod - y sees it. How
A
D
E
your sweet smile has a way of light - ing up a room.
A
F♯m
E
Yeah, you shine like dia - monds in
(You
D
A/C♯
B
ev - 'ry - thing you do. Oh,
shine like dia - monds do.)

A
D
E
love, love, love's look - in' good, good, good on you.
1.
2.
A
D
E
A
Female:
I
Bridge:
F♯m
B
knew right a - way from the ver - y first kiss that it does-n't get much bet - ter than this. We
(Love's kiss.)
D
E
A
E/G♯
fit just like a fa - v'rite pair of jeans.

F♯m B

We just keep com-ing back for more_ like two kids in a can - dy store._ And
(For more.)

D E

now I know_ what ev - 'ry - bod - y means_ when they_ say..._

Chorus:

M:

A7 D E

Love, love,_ love's look-in' good, good, good_ on_ you.

f *Honky-tonk style*

A7 G F♯m Em D E

Can you feel it? Oh, ev - 'ry-bod - y sees it. How

A
D
E
your sweet smile has a way of light - ing up a room.
A
F♯m
E
Yeah, you shine like dia - monds in
(You
D
A/C♯
B
ev - 'ry - thing you do.
shine like dia - monds do.)
Oh,
A
D
E
love, love, love's look - in' good, good, good on you.

A
D
E
Well, I'm tell - in' you, might-y, might-y good, babe.
M:
Love, love, love's look - in' good, good, good on you.
F:
Love's look - in' good on you, oh.
A7
N.C.
Love, love, love's look-in' good, good, good on you.

HOME IS WHERE THE HEART IS

Words and Music by
DAVE HAYWOOD, CHARLES KELLEY,
HILLARY SCOTT and VICTORIA SHAW

Verse 1 (sing 1st time only):

Female:

D / E♭ — G(9) / A♭(9) — Em7 / Fm7 — A7sus / B♭7sus

1. I felt I was spin-ning my wheels. Be - fore too long, the road was call - ing.

Verse 2 (sing 2nd time only):

worked third shift at an all - night din - er. On - ly stayed to save a lit - tle mon - ey for

D / E♭ — G(9) / A♭(9) — Em7 / Fm7 — A7sus / B♭7sus

I packed ev - 'ry-thing I owned, so sure that I was leav - ing this

e-nough gas to make it to the east coast. That's when I saw the bright - est pair of

D / E♭ — G(9) / A♭(9) — Em7 / Fm7 — A7sus / B♭7sus

small town life be - hind for good__ and not a sin - gle tear was fall - ing.

deep blue eyes walk - ing straight in - to my life.____

Bm
Cm
G(9)
A♭(9)
It took leav - ing for me to un - der - stand,
And ev - 'ry night we talked till it be - came so clear.
Bm
Cm
1.
To Next Strain
A
B♭
some - times your dreams just aren't what life has planned.
And I could feel those dreams in -
cresc.
2.
A
B♭
Both:
side shift - ing gears, 'cause love brought me here.
cresc.

Chorus:
D
D/F#
G(9)
Asus
E♭
Both:
E♭/G
A♭(9)
F:
B♭sus
Ma - ma said, "Home is where the heart is," when I left that town.
f
D
D/F#
G(9)
Asus
E♭
Both:
E♭/G
A♭(9)
F:
B♭sus
I made it all the way to West Vir - gin - ia, and that's where my heart found
Bm
A
G
D/F#
Cm
B♭
A♭
Both:
E♭/G
ex - act - ly where I'm s'posed to be. It did - n't take much
Em7
A
Fm7
B♭
time, it's just south of the Ma - son - Dix - on line.

D
G(9)
Em
A7sus
E♭
A♭(9)
Fm
B♭7sus
Just south of the Ma - son - Dix - on line.
1.
D.S. 𝄋
D
G(9)
E♭
A♭(9)
Em
Fm
A7sus
B♭7sus
2. I
dim.
2.
Em
A
Fm
B♭
Bridge:
Bm
Cm
F:
And I'm stand - ing in my
Em7
Fm7
Both:
G
A♭
A
B♭
veil a - bout to say, "I do," as Ma-ma smiles with tear - drops in her eyes.

D / E♭ — Bm / Cm

F: And then, I re - al - ize there's

Em7 / Fm7 — C / D♭ — G/B / A♭/C

some-thing Ma - ma al - ways knew: **Both:** Love is what I real - ly left to find.

A / B♭

dim.

Chorus:

D / E♭ — D/F♯ / E♭/G

mp

F: She said, "Home is where the heart

G(9) / A♭(9) — Asus / B♭sus — D / E♭ — D/F♯ / E♭/G

is," when I left that town. **Both:** I made it all the way to West Vir - gin -

cresc. poco a poco

G(9)
Asus
Bm
A
A♭(9)
B♭sus
Cm
B♭
F:
ia, and that's where my heart found ex-act-ly where I'm s'posed to be.
f
G
D/F♯
Em7
A♭
Both:
E♭/G
Fm7
It did-n't take much time,
A
D
G(9)
B♭
E♭
A♭(9)
it's just south of the Ma-son-Dix-on line.
Em
A7sus
D
G(9)
Fm
B♭7sus
E♭
A♭(9)
Just south of the Ma-son-Dix-on line, line.

Em
Fm
A7sus
B♭7sus
D
E♭
D/F♯
E♭/G
Male:
Ma - ma said, "Home is where_ the
G(9)
A♭(9)
Asus
B♭sus
M:
heart is."
F:
It's just south of the Ma - son - Dix - on line.___
Ma - ma said, "Home is where_ the
Both:
heart is."
F: It's just south of the Ma - son - Dix - on line,
N.C.
line.

THINGS PEOPLE SAY

Words and Music by
CHARLES KELLEY and DAVE HAYWOOD

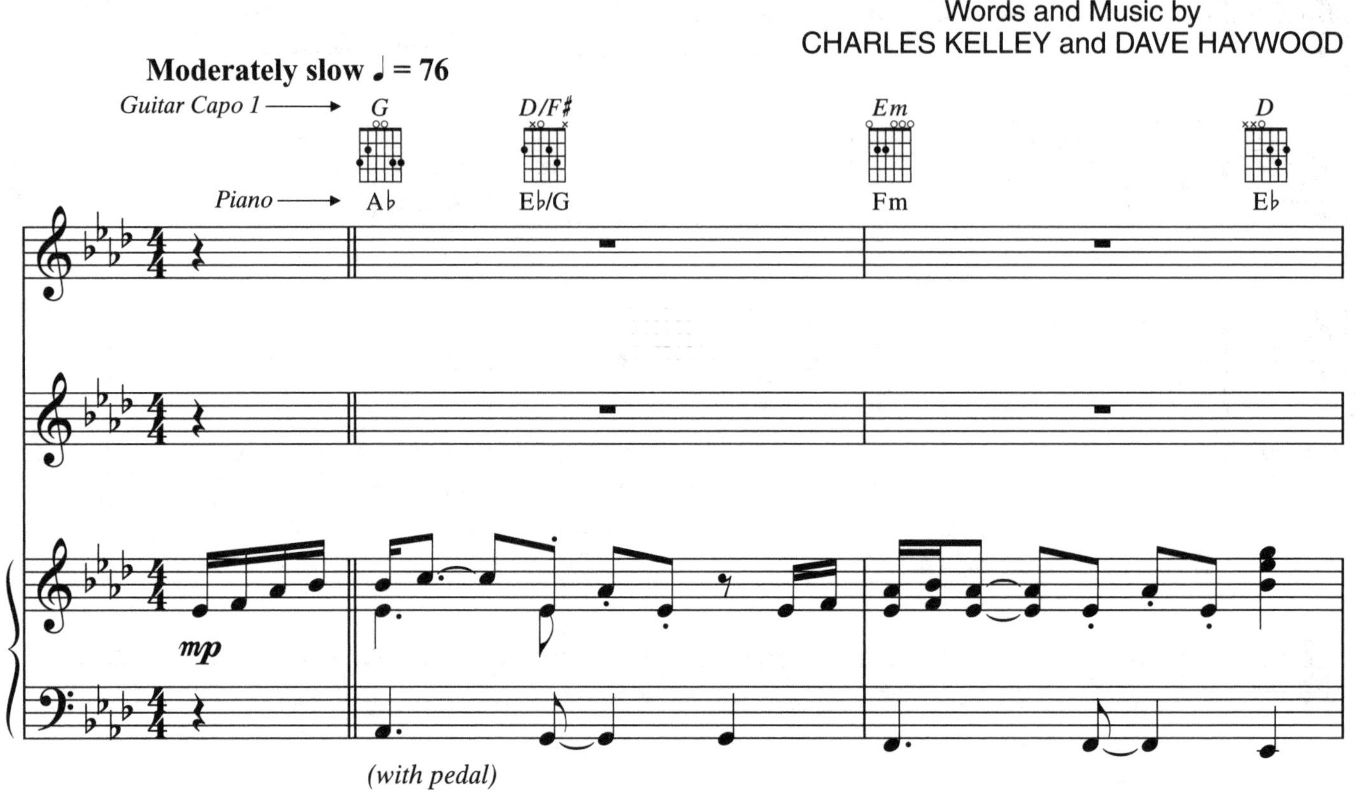

Verse 1 (sing 1st time only):
G
D/F♯
Em
D
A♭
E♭/G
Fm
E♭
1. There I was at the bus stop beg - gin' you just to stay; can we
Verse 2 (sing 2nd time only):
2. The preach-er stopped by the house last Tues - day, asked if I was fine. We sat and
C
C(9)
Dsus
D
D♭
D♭(9)
E♭sus
E♭
work this out? Ba - by, we can work this out.
talked a while. He tried to make me smile. But
G
D/F♯
Em
D
A♭
E♭/G
Fm
E♭
A dust trail from a Grey-hound head - ed for the west coast; as I
it's so hard to show my face 'round late - ly in this small town. I guess they

C
D
Db
Eb
watch you leave it's get - ting hard to breathe. No, this ain't
heard the news a - bout me and you. It's three A.
C
C(9)
D
Db
Db(9)
Eb
how it was sup - posed to be. If
M. and I can't sleep at all. I
C/E
D/F#
Db/F
Eb/G
you're out chas - ing all your dreams, tell me, where does that leave me?
won - der where you are to - night and do I ev - er cross your mind.

Chorus:
G
A♭
C(9)
D♭(9)
What a-bout the plans_ that you left be - hind?_ The lit - tle white house_ by the rail-way line, the
mf
D
E♭
Am
B♭m
G/D
A♭/E♭
C
D♭
D
E♭
one_ we picked_ out,_ we e-ven put the pay-ment down?_ And
G
A♭
C(9)
D♭(9)
what a-bout the prom - ise that_ you made_ to stay_ with me_ 'til your dy-ing day,_ said you'd
D
E♭
Am
B♭m
G/D
A♭/E♭
Am/C
B♭m/D♭
nev - er go a - way? Are they just things that peo - ple say?_

1.
G
D/F#
Em
D
A♭
E♭/G
Fm
E♭
Are they just things,
dim.
C
Dsus
D
2.
G
D♭
E♭sus
E♭
A♭
ba - by?
Well, my
cresc.
Bridge:
C(9)
D
D♭(9)
E♭
mom - ma won't stop cry - ing.
She won - ders what went wrong.
Could I have
C/E
D/F#
D♭/F
E♭/G
loved a lit - tle deep - er,
or did I hold on too strong?
Ooo.

Guitar solo:

G / A♭ — C(9) / D♭(9)

D / E♭ — Am / B♭m — G/B / A♭/C — D / E♭ — D/E / E♭/F

Whoa, no.

Chorus:

A / B♭ — D(9) / E♭(9)

What a-bout the plans that you left be-hind? The lit - tle white house by the rail-way line, the

E / F — Bm / Cm — A/C♯ / B♭/D — D / E♭ — E / F

one we picked out, we e-ven put the pay-ment down? And

A
B♭
D(9)
E♭(9)
what a-bout the prom - ise that__ you made__ to stay___ with me__ 'til your dy-ing day,__ said you'd
E
F
Bm
Cm
A/E
B♭/F
Bm/D
Cm/E♭
nev - er go___ a - way?______ Are they just things that peo - ple say?__
A
B♭
E/G♯
F/A
F♯m
Gm
E
F
Whoa,______ are they just things,_
mf
D
E♭
A/C♯
B♭/D
Bm
Cm
E/G♯
F/A
A
B♭
______ ba - by?______ Ooh.

SLOW DOWN SISTER

Words and Music by
DAVE HAYWOOD, CHARLES KELLEY,
HILLARY SCOTT and JASON GAMBILL

Slow Down Sister - 5 - 1
33437

C G C G D
ing, I'm not fall - ing in love with you. I play by my rules
zy, that I'm cra - zy for a - void - ing you, but, hon - ey, I've got my free -
G C G C G
and, be - lieve me, you don't want me too close to you.
dom and my rea - sons, all the rea - sons for what I do.
D Em7 D/F#
And e - ven though you look so fine, I've been
But that last kiss just did me in, and I don't
C(9) Cm
on this bro - ken road one too man - y times.
wan - na look at you as some - thing more than just a friend.

Chorus:
Both:
G C G C G
Slow down, sis - ter, 'cause I just can't love you, but I just can't get you off my
D G C G
mind. Oh, and Lord knows I need you, but I just don't wan - na put this
C G 1. D G 2. D
rust - ed heart up on the line. 2. I've heard peo - ple say line.
Bridge:
G C G C M: G C G C Female:
Whoa, slow down, sis - ter. I've got to

G
C
G
C
M:
make_ you mine.
All I'm ask - in' for is just a lit - tle
D
G
C
G
time,
a lit-tle more_ time.
(Inst. solo ad lib....
C
G
D
G
C
G
C
G
D
G
Chorus:
N.C.
Both:
...end solo)
So, slow down, sis - ter, 'cause I just can't love you, but I

D5
G
just can't get you off my mind.
Oh, and Lord___ knows I need you, but I
C
G
D
Male:
just don't wan-na put this rust - ed heart up on the line.
Slow down, sis -
Both:
ter.
Would you slow_
M:
___down, slow_down, slow___down
just_one time.
rit.

CAN'T TAKE MY EYES OFF YOU

Words and Music by
DAVE HAYWOOD, CHARLES KELLEY
and HILLARY SCOTT

Verse:

G Em7

know ___ that the bridg - es that I've burned a - long ___ the
love ___ when you tell me that I'm pret - ty when I just wake

Am7 D(4)

way ___ have left ___ me ___
up. ___ And I ___ love ___

G Em7

___ with these walls and these scars that won't go a -
___ when you tease me when I'm mood - y, but it's nev - er too

Am7 D D2

way. ___
much. ___

F(9)
E
And o - pen - ing up has
I'm fall - ing fast, but the
3
Am
Am(maj7)
Am7
Am6
al - ways been the hard - est thing
truth is, I'm not scared at all.
Dm7
Gsus
G
un - til you came.
You climbed my walls.
So,
Chorus:
C
Am7
Both:
lay here be - side me. Just hold me and don't let

Fmaj7
G
go.
This
C
Am7
feel - ing I'm feel - ing is some - thing I've nev - er
Fmaj7
Gsus
G
known.
And I just can't
F(9)
C(9)/E
Dm7
C(9)
take my eyes off you.
And I just can't

F(9)
C(9)/E
1.
B♭6
take my eyes off you.
D7sus
D
2.
B♭6
2. I
you,
F/A
B♭6
off
you,
F/A
B♭6
off
you,

F/A Asus

cresc.

Chorus:

A D

So, lay here be - side me. Just

Bm7 G

hold me and don't let go.

A D

Oh, this feel - ing I'm feel - ing is

Bm7
G
some - thing I've nev - er known.
G(9)
D(9)/F♯
And I just can't take my eyes off
Em7
D
G(9)
D(9)/F♯
you. And I just can't take my eyes off
F
C/E
D
you.
decresc.
mp

ONE DAY YOU WILL

Gtr. tuned down 1/2 step:
⑥ = E♭ ③ = G♭
⑤ = A♭ ② = B♭
④ = D♭ ① = E♭

Words and Music by
DAVE HAYWOOD, CHARLES KELLEY,
HILLARY SCOTT and CLAY MILLS

E
F♯m7(4)
A2
E♭
Fm7(4)
A♭2
Male:
1. You
Verse:
feel like you're fall - ing back - wards, like you're slip - pin' through the cracks.
wake up ev - 'ry morn - ing and ask your-self, "What am I do-ing here,
an - y - way?"
Both:
Like no
With the weight
M:
Both:
one would e - ven no - tice if you left this town and nev-er came
of all those dis - ap - point-ments whis-per-ing in your

1. E
F♯m7(4)
A2
To Next Strain
2. E
E♭
Fm7(4)
A♭2
back.
You walk out - side
ear.
And you're just bare -
B
B♭
and all you see is rain,
you look in - side
and all you feel is pain.
ly hang - ing by a thread,
you wan - na scream,
but you're down to your last breath.
C♯m7
D
Cm7
D♭
And you can't see it now.
And you don't know it yet.
But
cresc.
Chorus:
E
A(9)
E♭
A♭(9)
down the road, the sun is shin - ing. In ev - 'ry cloud, there's a sil - ver lin - ing.
mf

C#m
Cm
B
B♭
A
A♭
Bsus
B♭sus
Just keep hold - ing on.
(Just keep hold - ing on.)
And
E
E♭
A(9)
A♭(9)
ev - 'ry heart - ache makes you strong - er, but it won't be much long - er. You'll find
C#m
Cm
B
B♭
A
A♭
E/G#
M: E♭/G
love, you'll find peace, and the "you" you're meant to be. I know right
A
A♭
1.
Bsus
B♭sus
Both:
now, that's not the way you feel, but one day you

E
F♯m7(4)
A2
D.S. 𝄋
E♭
Fm7(4)
A♭2
will.
2. You
dim.
2.
Bridge:
Bsus
F♯m7
E/G♯
B♭sus
Fm7
E♭/G
Both:
Female:
but one day you will find
A
E/B
F♯m7
E/G♯
A♭
E♭/B♭
Fm7
E♭/G
Both:
F:
the strength to rise a - bove. You will find
Am
A♭m
just what you're made of, you're made of.

Chorus:
F♯
B(9)
Both:
F
B♭(9)
down the road, the sun is shining. In ev-'ry cloud, there's a silver lining.
D♯m
C♯
B
C♯sus
Dm
C
B♭
Csus
Just keep holding on. And
(Just keep holding on.)
F♯
B(9)
F
B♭(9)
ev-'ry heartache makes you stronger, but it won't be much longer. You'll find
D♯m
C♯
B
F♯/A♯
Dm
C
B♭
M:
F/A
love, you'll find peace, and the "you" you're meant to be. I know right

B(9)
B♭(9)
F:
now, that's not the way you feel, I know right
C♯7sus
C7sus
Both:
now that's not the way you feel, but one day you
dim.
F♯
F
G♯m7
Gm7
B(9)
B♭(9)
will. One day you
mf
F♯
F
G♯m7
Gm7
B(9)
B♭(9)
M:
will.
Oh, one day you will.

LADY ANTEBELLUM

WWW.LADYANTEBELLUM.COM

WWW.CAPITOLNASHVILLE.COM